In Celebration of:

Thoughts:

Name:

Thoughts:

Name:

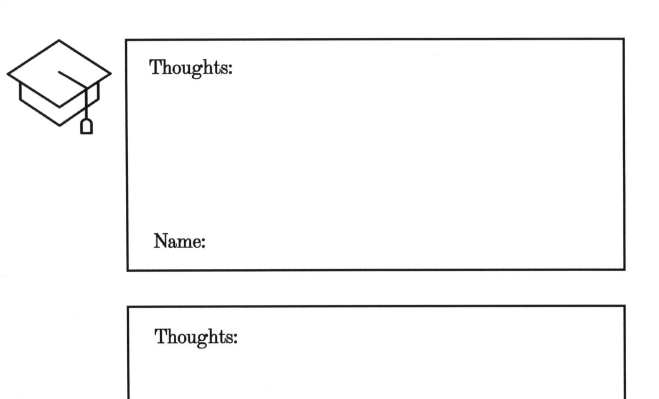

Thoughts:

Name:

Thoughts:

Name:

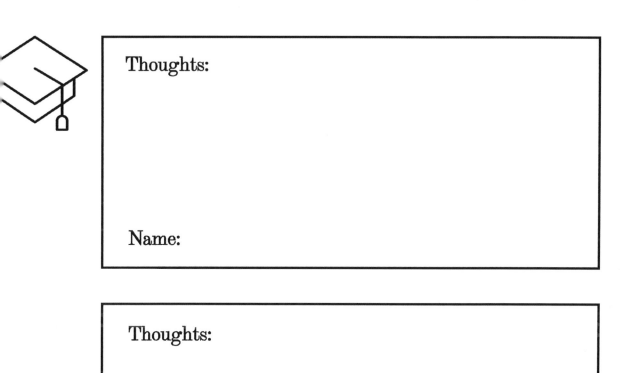

Thoughts:

Name:

Thoughts:

Name:

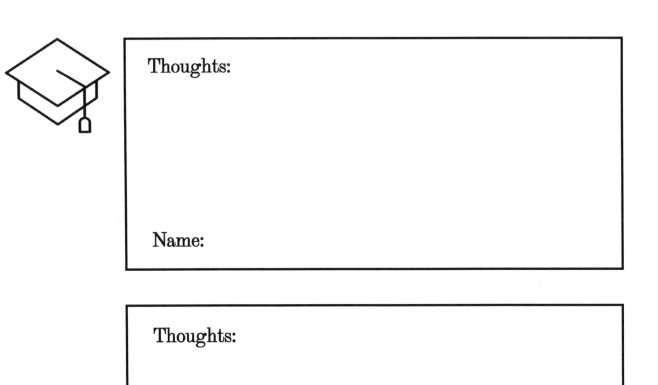

Thoughts:

Name:

Thoughts:

Name:

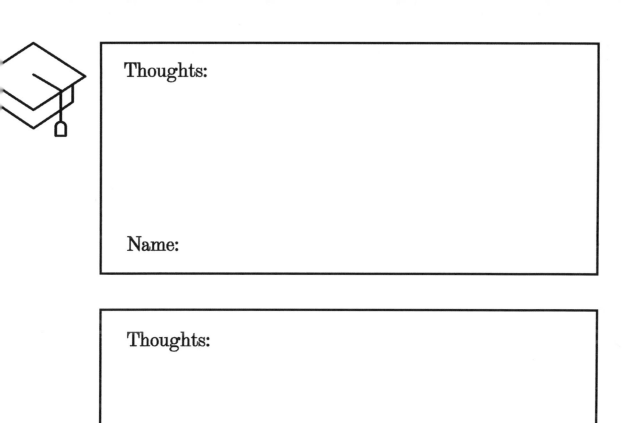

Thoughts:

Name:

Thoughts:

Name:

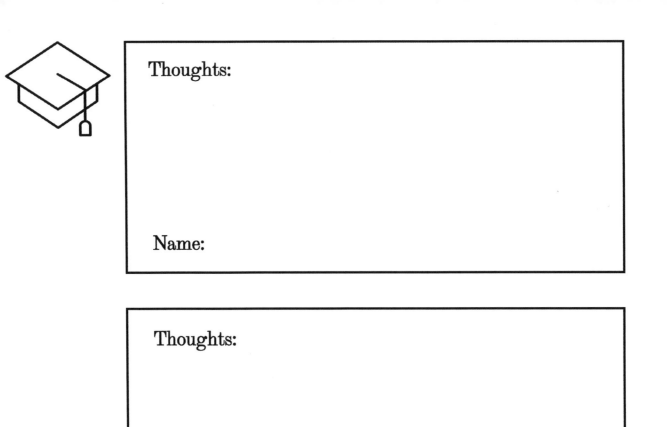

Thoughts:

Name:

Thoughts:

Name:

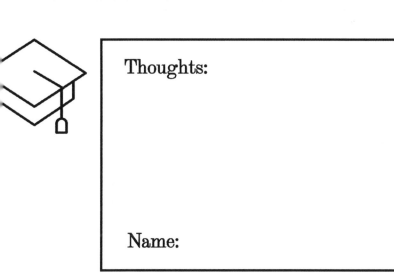

Thoughts:

Name:

Thoughts:

Name:

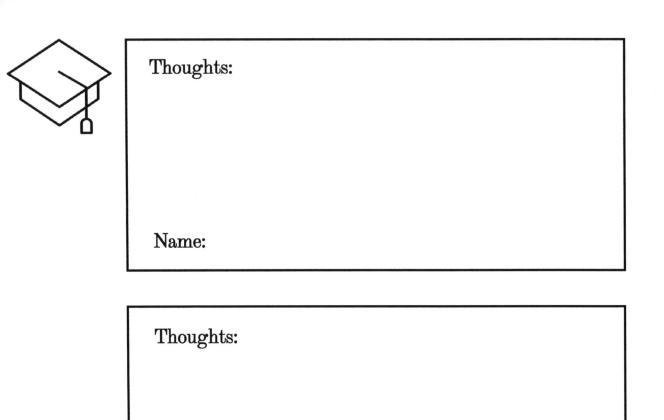

Thoughts:

Name:

Thoughts:

Name:

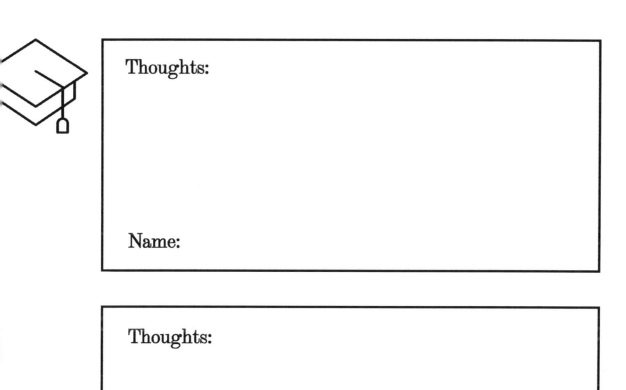

Thoughts:

Name:

Thoughts:

Name:

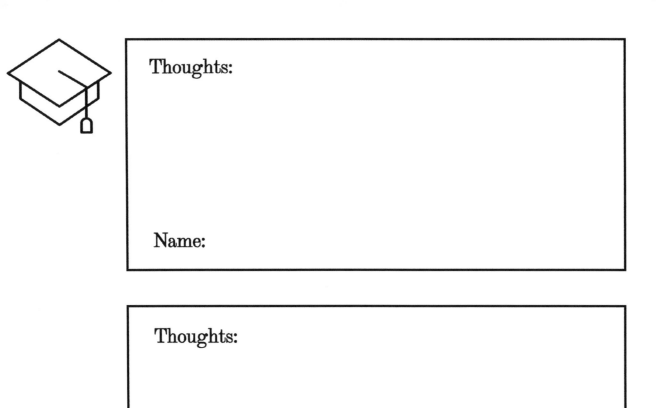

Thoughts:

Name:

Thoughts:

Name:

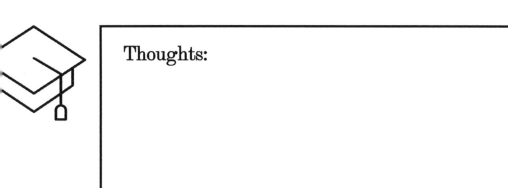

Thoughts:

Name:

Thoughts:

Name:

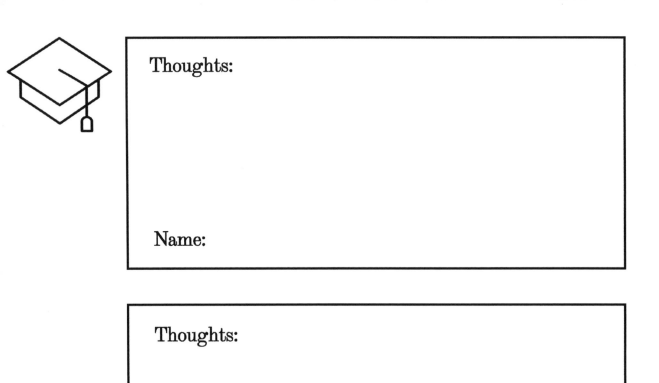

Thoughts:

Name:

Thoughts:

Name:

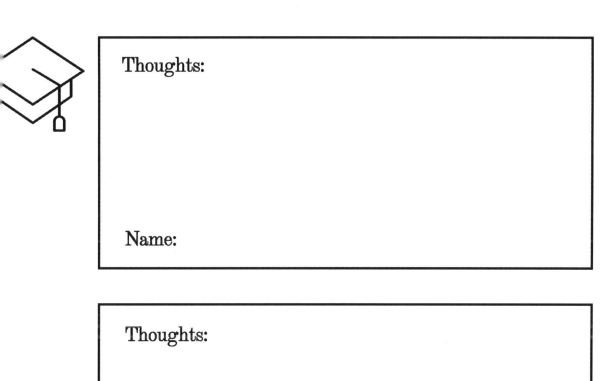

Thoughts:

Name:

Thoughts:

Name:

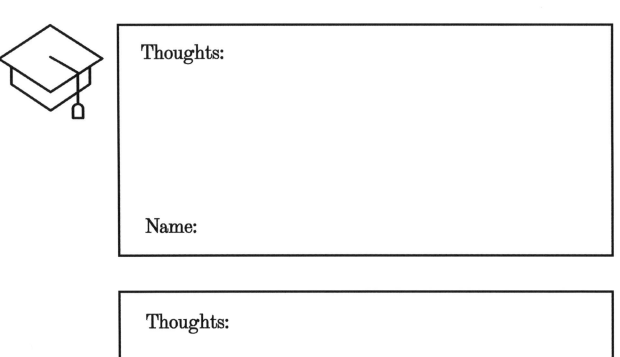

Thoughts:

Name:

Thoughts:

Name:

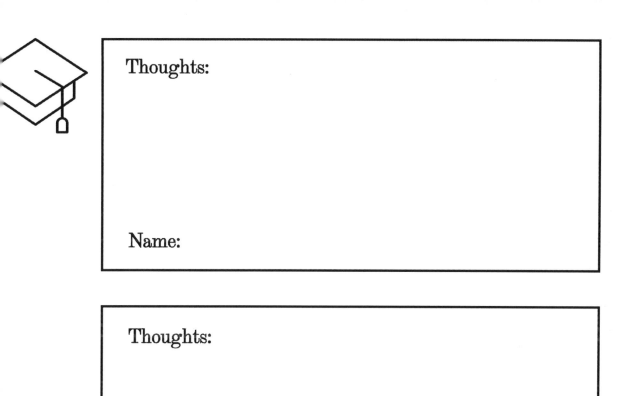

Thoughts:

Name:

Thoughts:

Name:

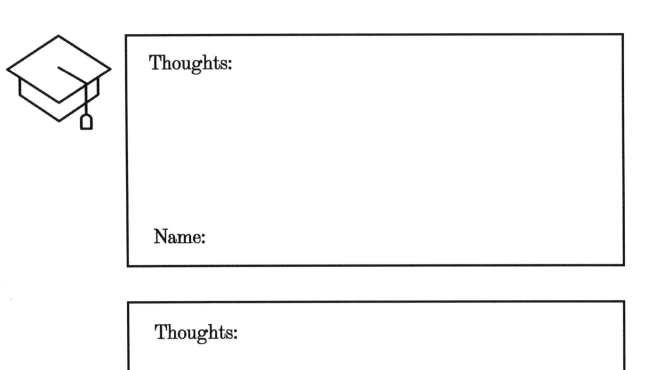

Thoughts:

Name:

Thoughts:

Name:

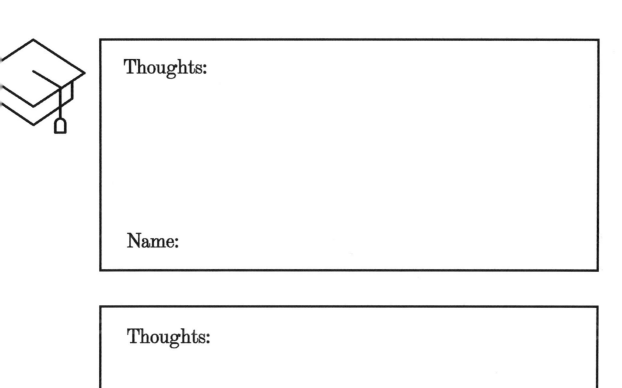

Thoughts:

Name:

Thoughts:

Name:

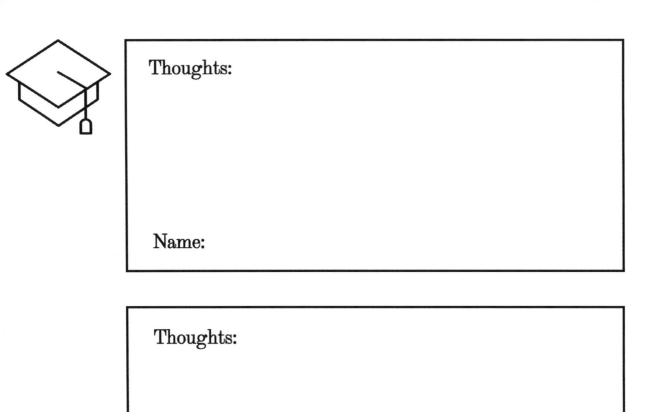

Thoughts:

Name:

Thoughts:

Name:

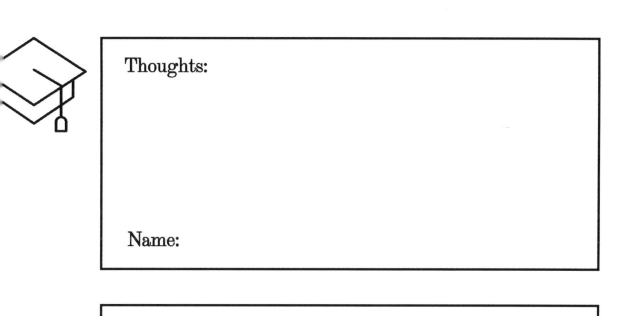

Thoughts:

Name:

Thoughts:

Name:

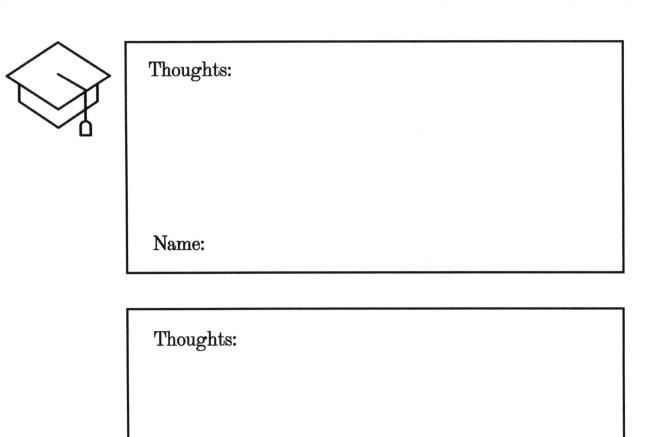

Thoughts:

Name:

Thoughts:

Name:

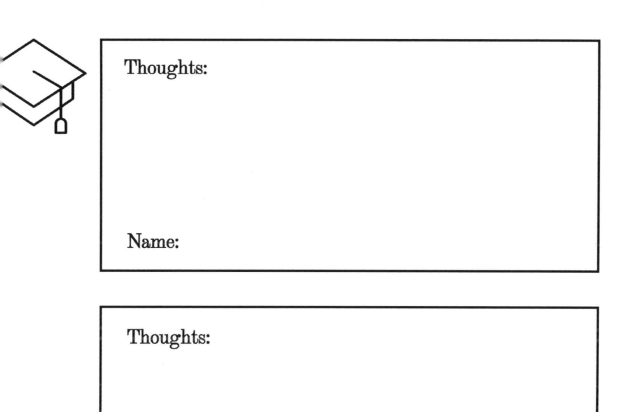

Thoughts:

Name:

Thoughts:

Name:

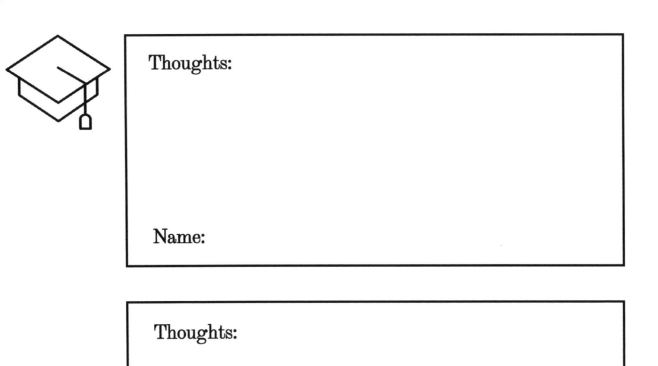

Thoughts:

Name:

Thoughts:

Name:

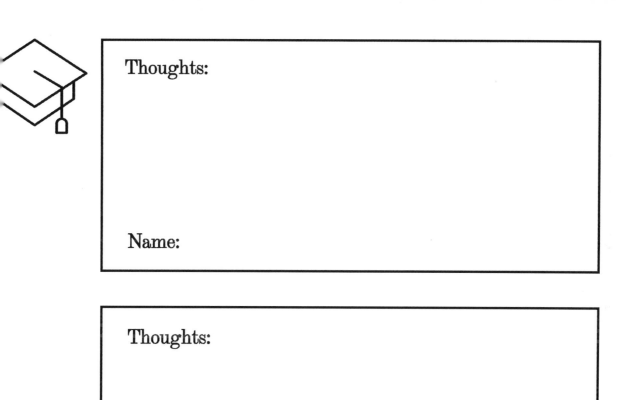

Thoughts:

Name:

Thoughts:

Name:

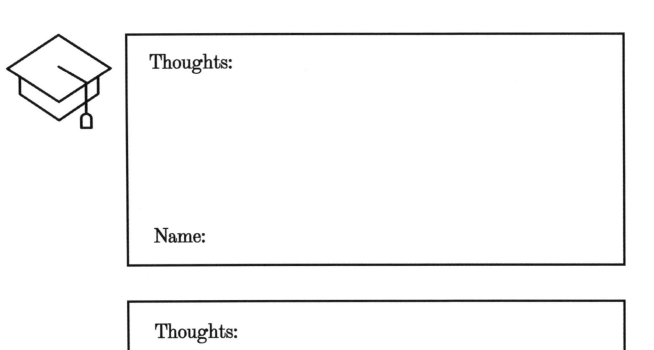

Thoughts:

Name:

Thoughts:

Name:

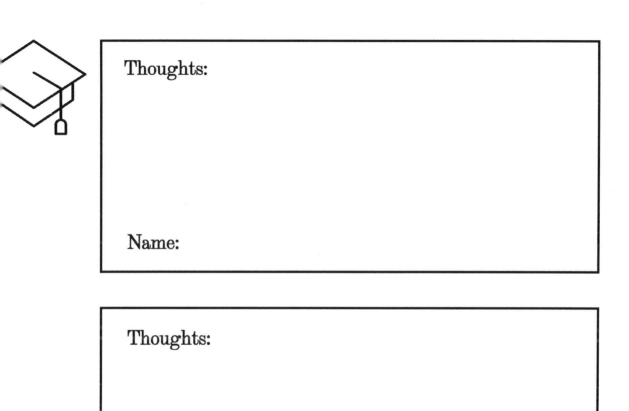

Thoughts:

Name:

Thoughts:

Name:

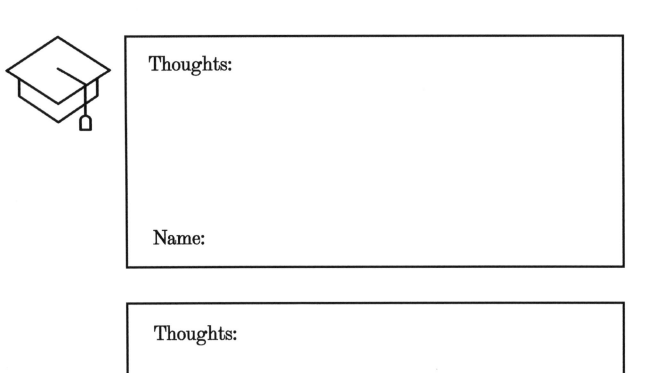

Thoughts:

Name:

Thoughts:

Name:

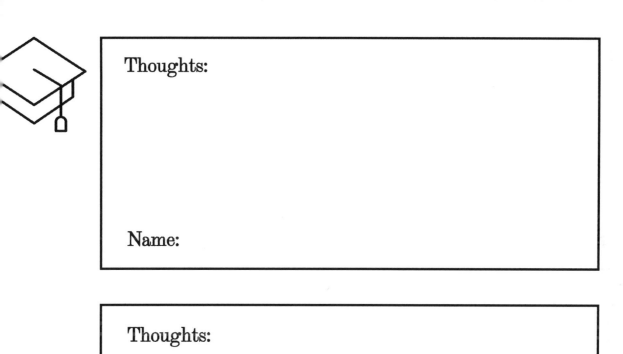

Thoughts:

Name:

Thoughts:

Name:

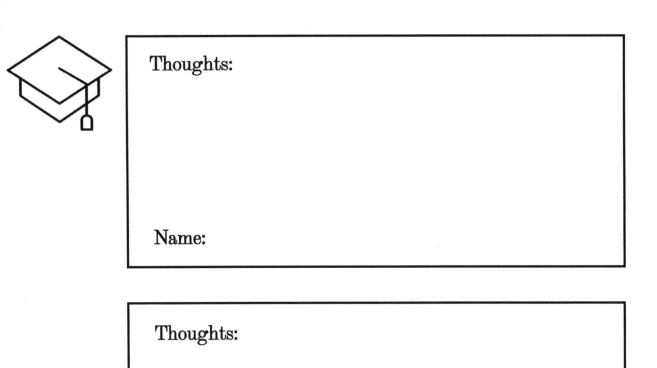

Thoughts:

Name:

Thoughts:

Name:

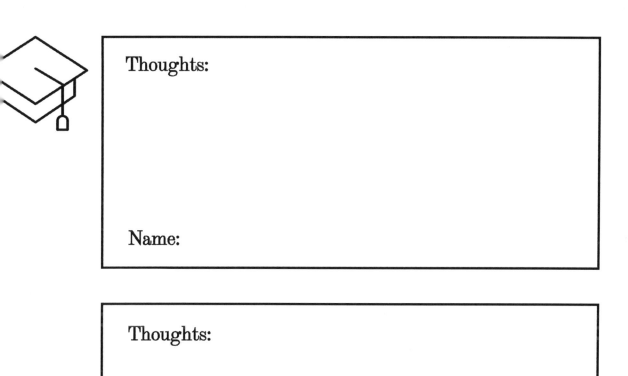

Thoughts:

Name:

Thoughts:

Name:

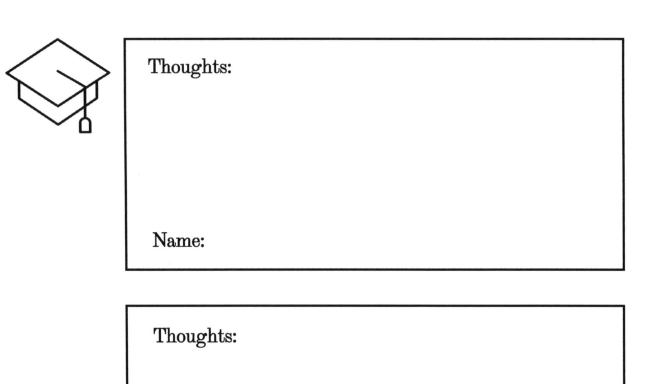

Thoughts:

Name:

Thoughts:

Name:

Thoughts:

Name:

Thoughts:

Name:

Thoughts:

Name:

Thoughts:

Name:

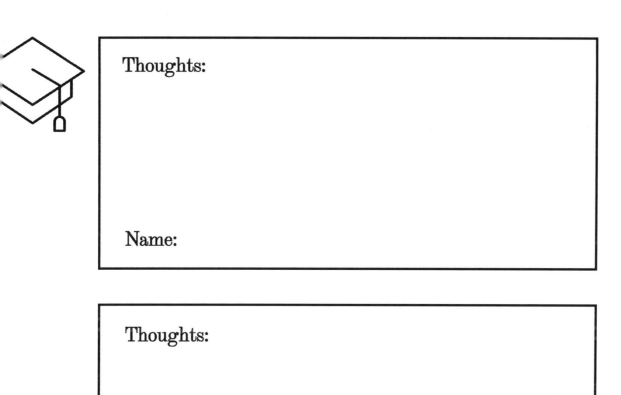

Thoughts:

Name:

Thoughts:

Name:

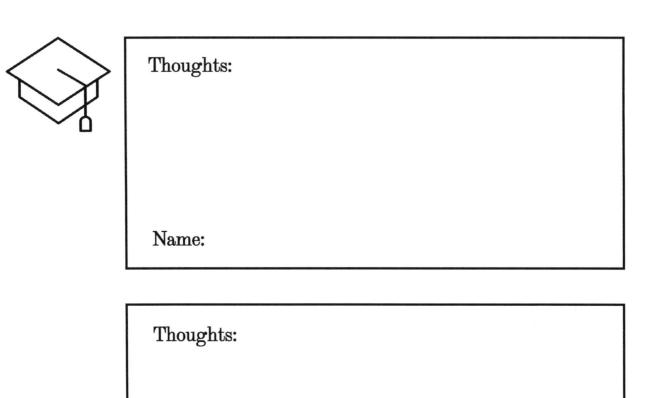

Thoughts:

Name:

Thoughts:

Name:

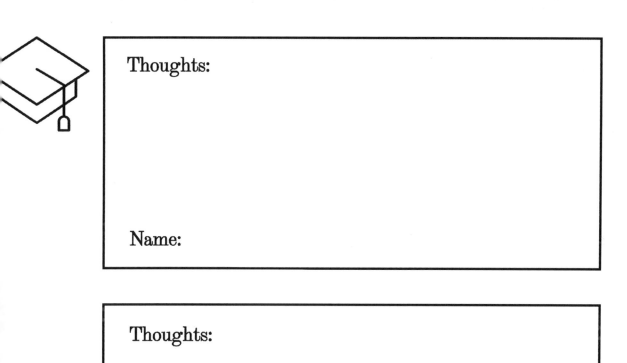

Thoughts:

Name:

Thoughts:

Name:

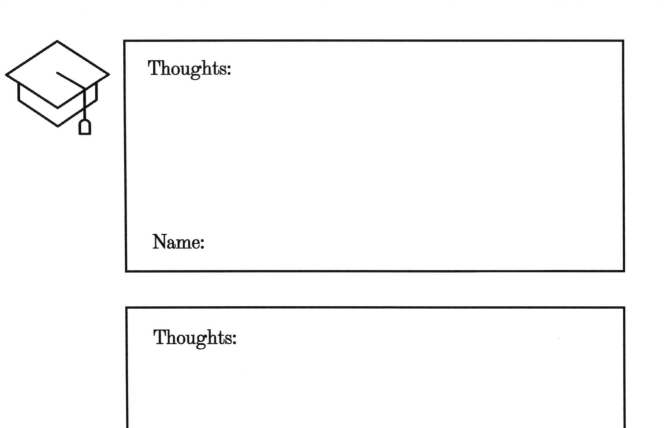

Thoughts:

Name:

Thoughts:

Name:

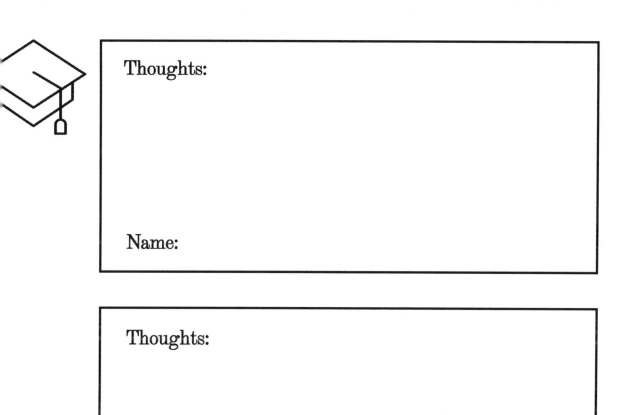

Thoughts:

Name:

Thoughts:

Name:

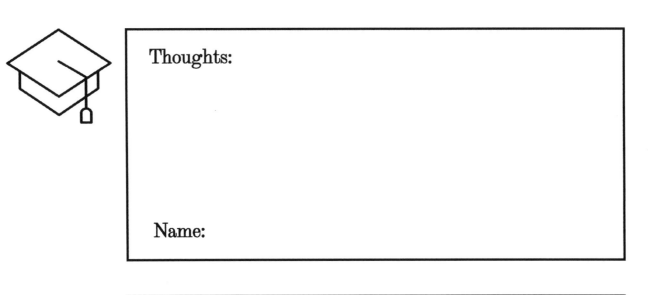

Thoughts:

Name:

Thoughts:

Name:

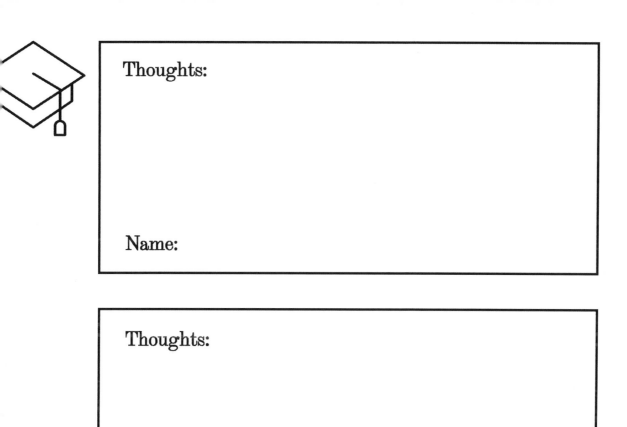

Thoughts:

Name:

Thoughts:

Name:

Thoughts:

Name:

Thoughts:

Name:

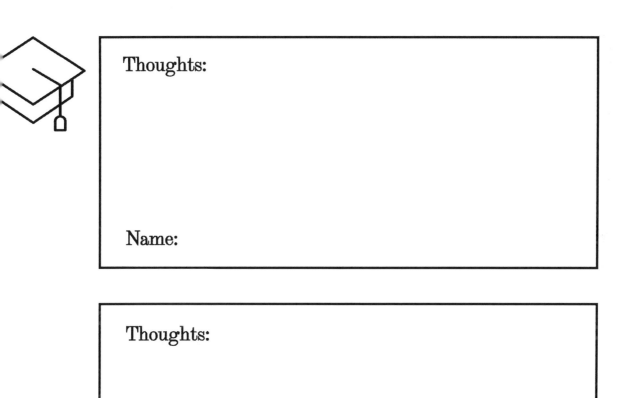

Thoughts:

Name:

Thoughts:

Name:

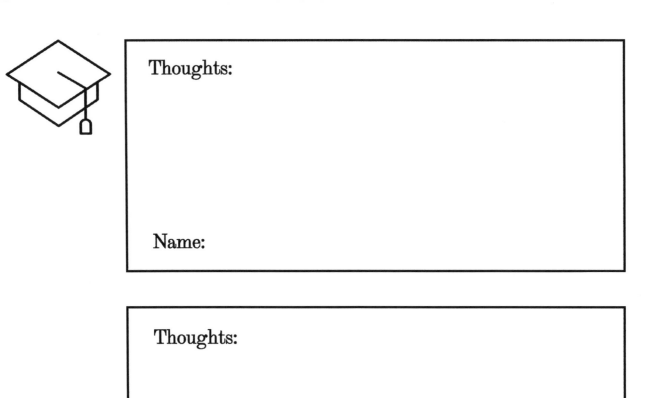

Thoughts:

Name:

Thoughts:

Name:

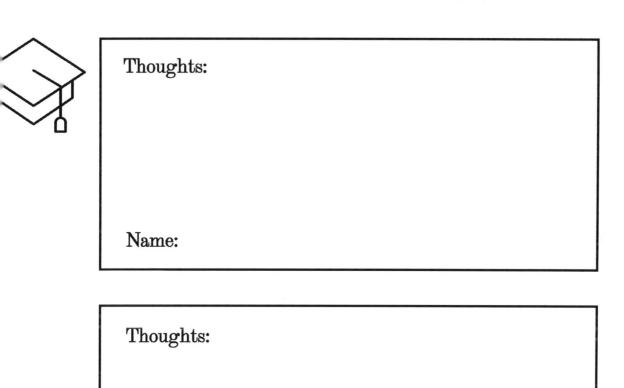

Thoughts:

Name:

Thoughts:

Name:

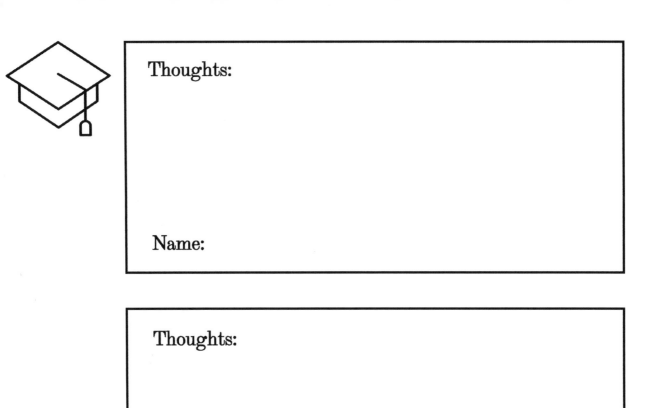

Thoughts:

Name:

Thoughts:

Name:

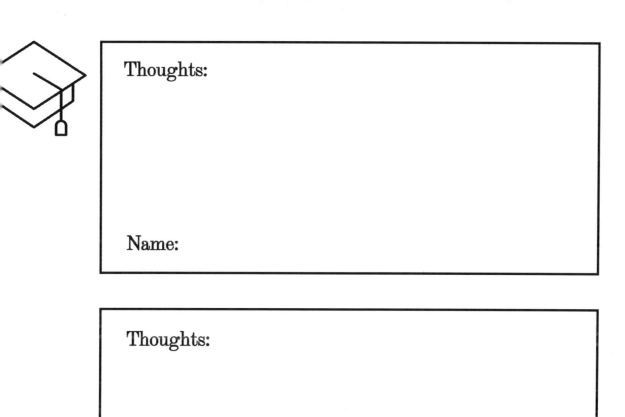

Thoughts:

Name:

Thoughts:

Name:

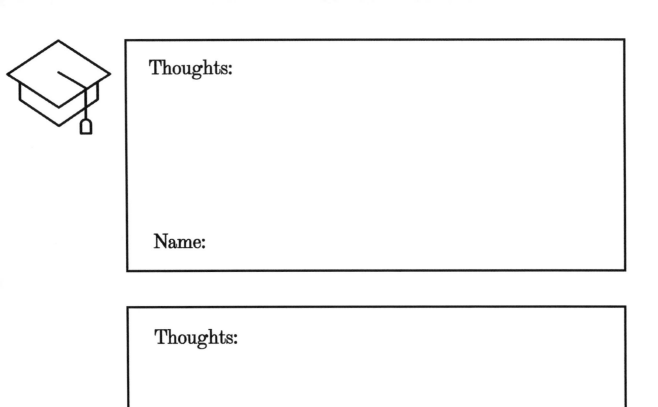

Thoughts:

Name:

Thoughts:

Name:

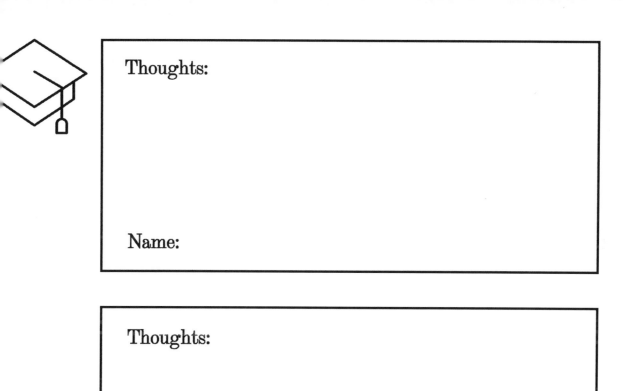

Thoughts:

Name:

Thoughts:

Name:

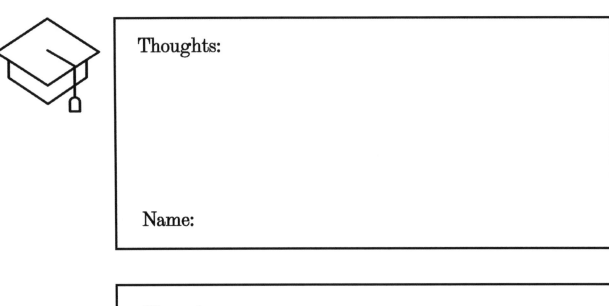

Thoughts:

Name:

Thoughts:

Name:

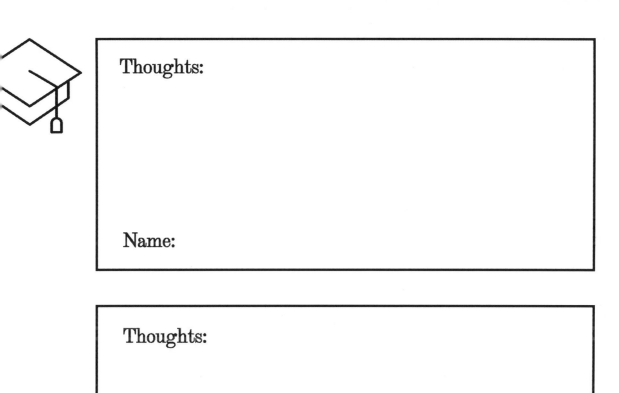

Thoughts:

Name:

Thoughts:

Name:

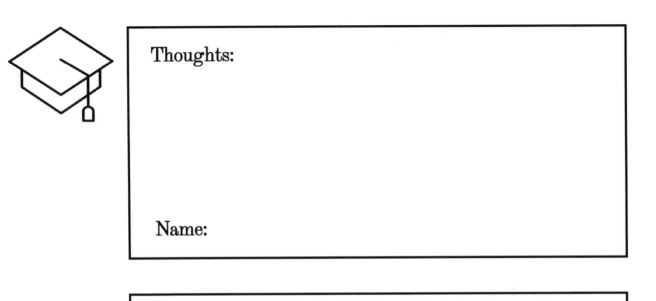

Thoughts:

Name:

Thoughts:

Name:

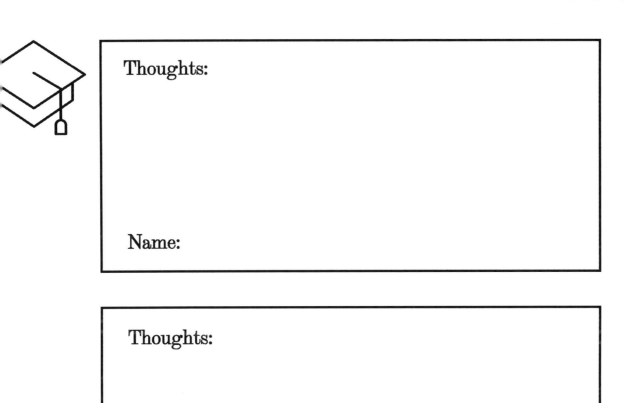

Thoughts:

Name:

Thoughts:

Name:

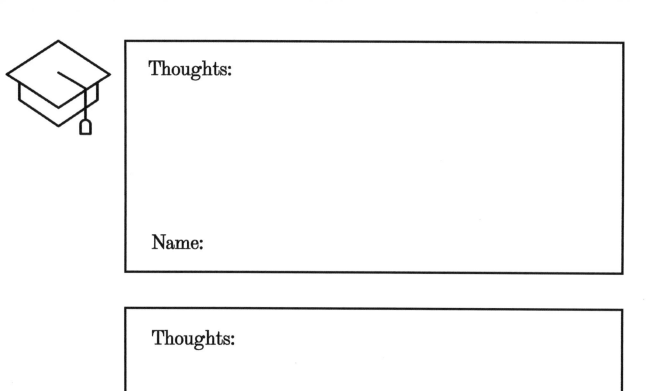

Thoughts:

Name:

Thoughts:

Name:

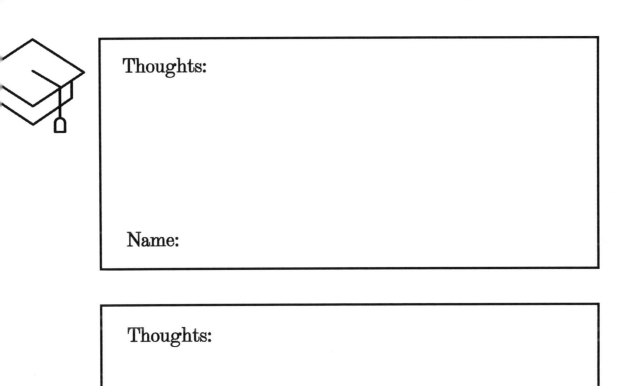

Thoughts:

Name:

Thoughts:

Name:

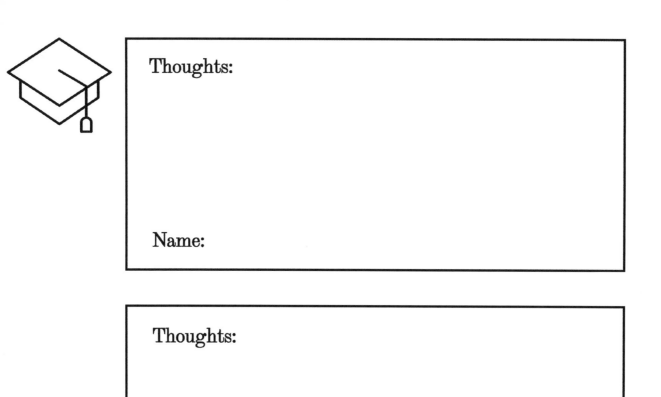

Thoughts:

Name:

Thoughts:

Name:

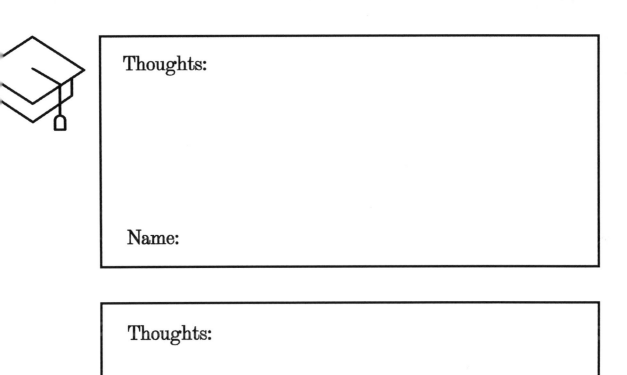

Thoughts:

Name:

Thoughts:

Name:

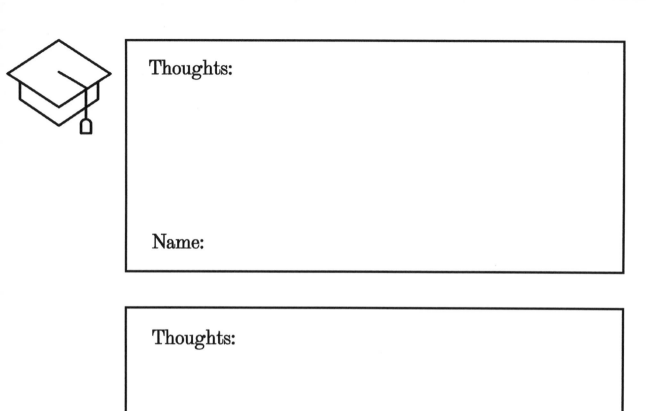

Thoughts:

Name:

Thoughts:

Name:

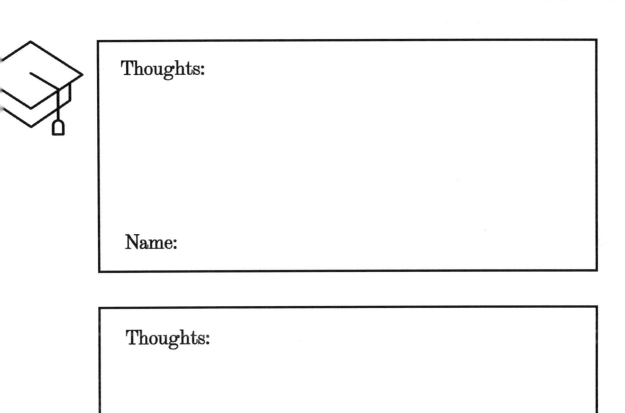

Thoughts:

Name:

Thoughts:

Name:

Thoughts:

Name:

Thoughts:

Name:

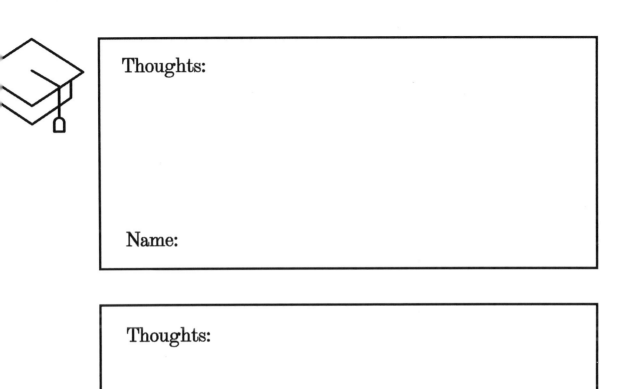

Thoughts:

Name:

Thoughts:

Name:

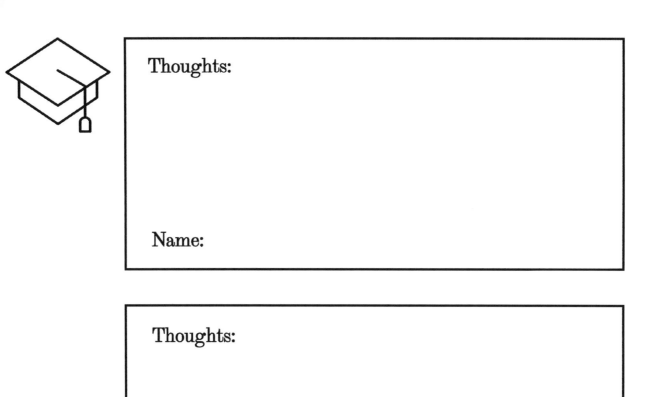

Thoughts:

Name:

Thoughts:

Name:

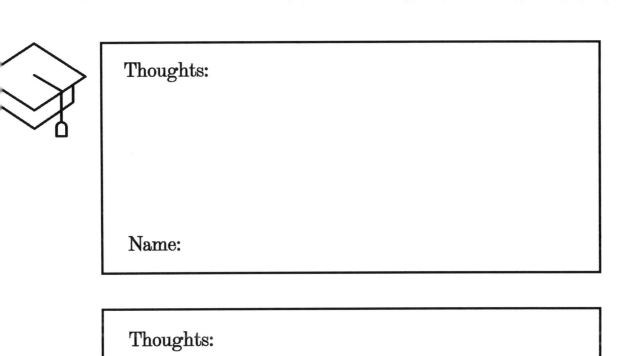

Thoughts:

Name:

Thoughts:

Name:

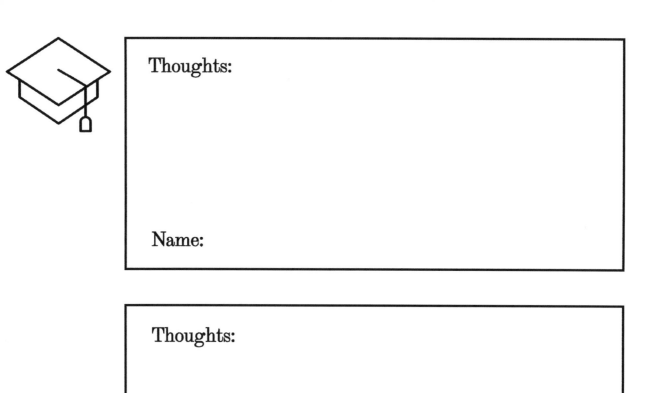

Thoughts:

Name:

Thoughts:

Name:

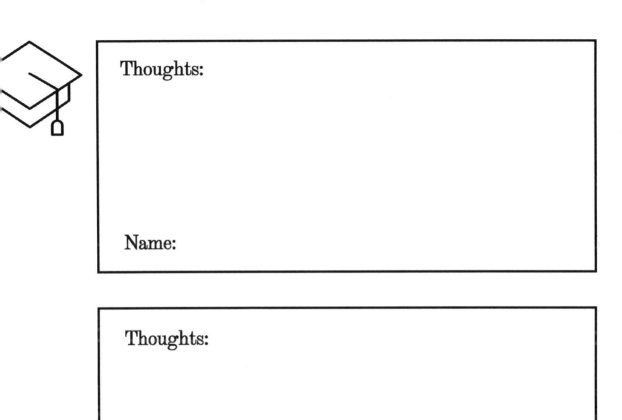

Thoughts:

Name:

Thoughts:

Name:

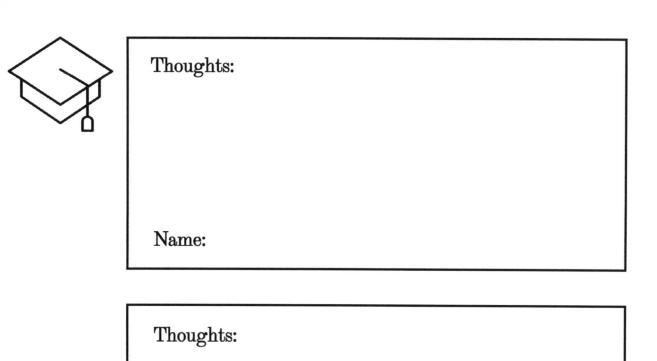

Thoughts:

Name:

Thoughts:

Name:

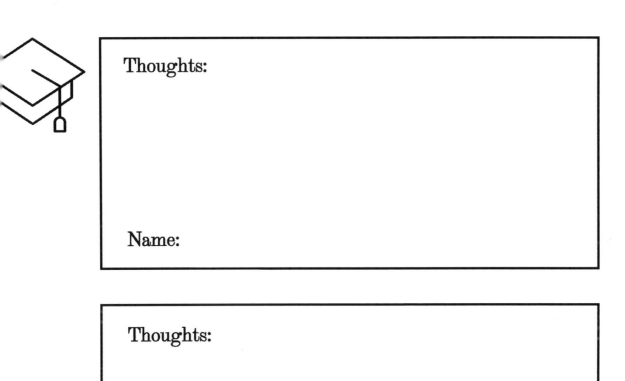

Thoughts:

Name:

Thoughts:

Name:

Thoughts:

Name:

Thoughts:

Name:

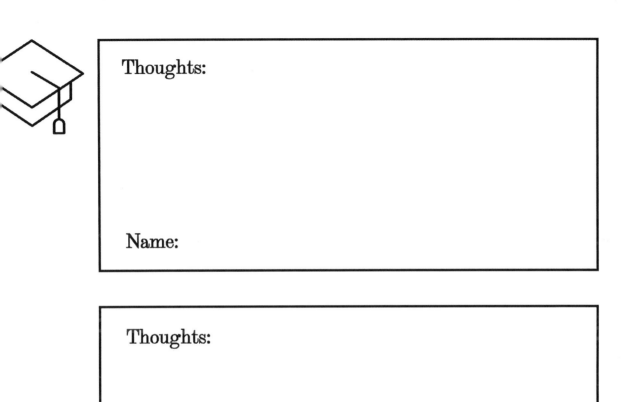

Thoughts:

Name:

Thoughts:

Name:

Thoughts:

Name:

Thoughts:

Name:

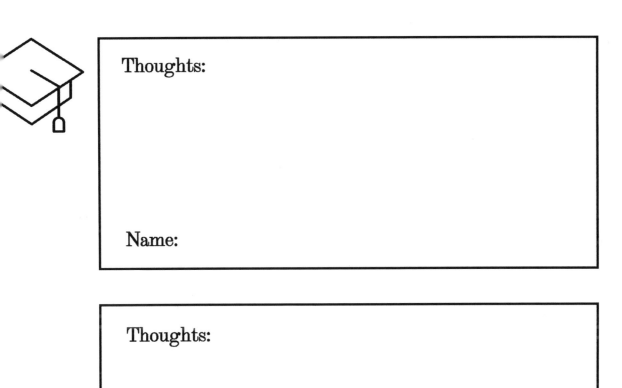

Thoughts:

Name:

Thoughts:

Name:

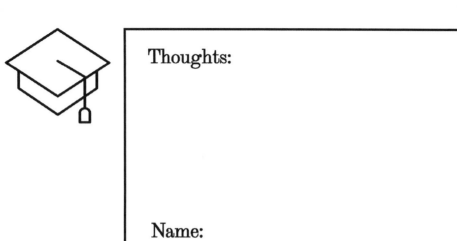

Thoughts:

Name:

Thoughts:

Name:

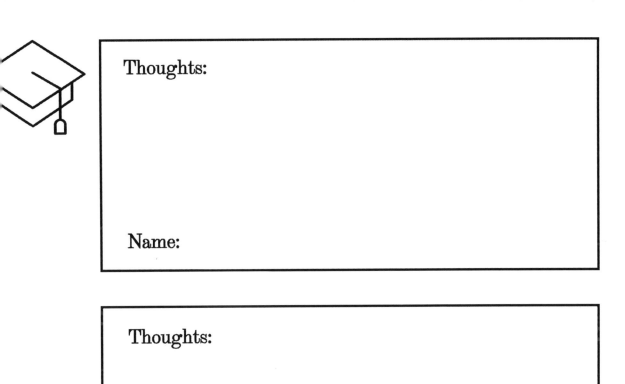

Thoughts:

Name:

Thoughts:

Name:

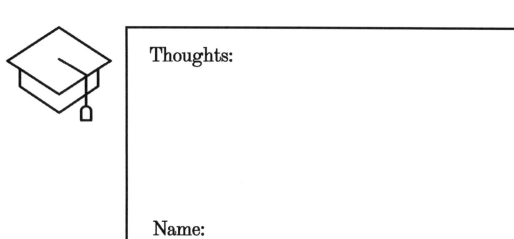

Thoughts:

Name:

Thoughts:

Name:

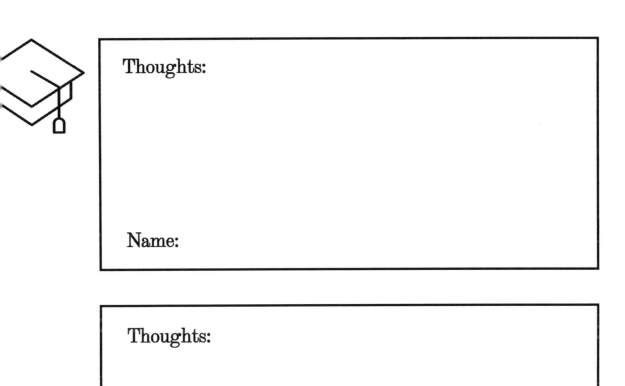

Thoughts:

Name:

Thoughts:

Name:

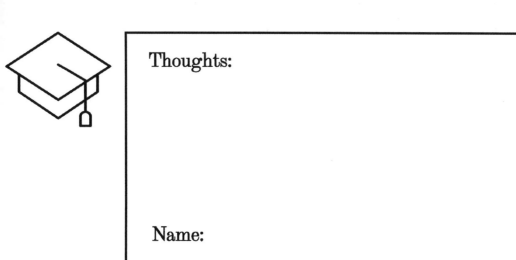

Thoughts:

Name:

Thoughts:

Name:

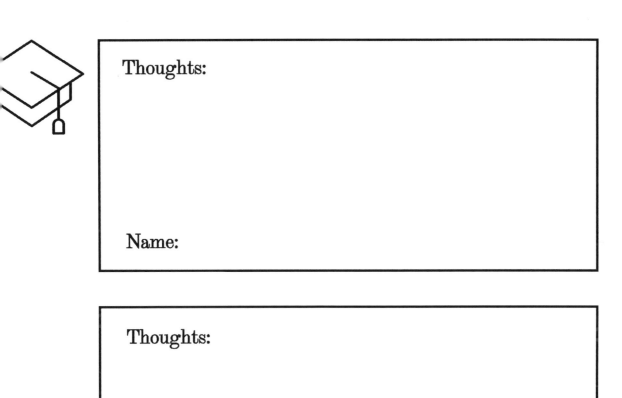

Thoughts:

Name:

Thoughts:

Name:

Thoughts:

Name:

Thoughts:

Name:

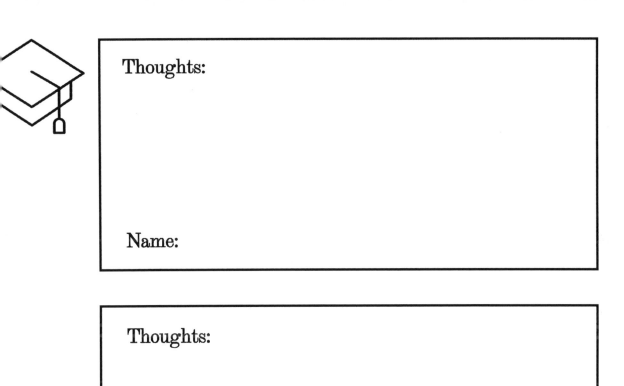

Thoughts:

Name:

Thoughts:

Name:

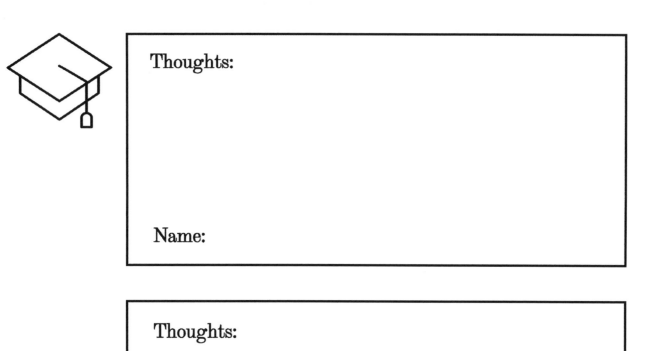

Thoughts:

Name:

Thoughts:

Name:

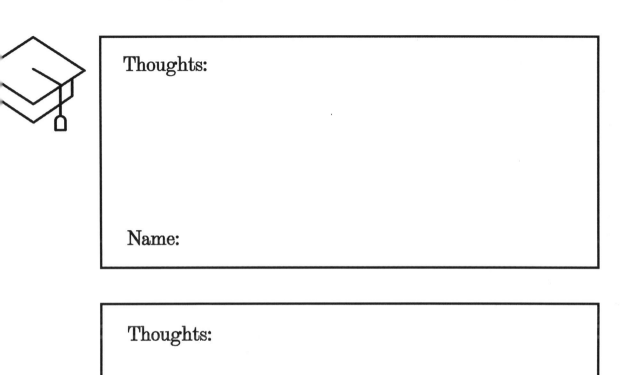

Thoughts:

Name:

Thoughts:

Name:

Thoughts:

Name:

Thoughts:

Name:

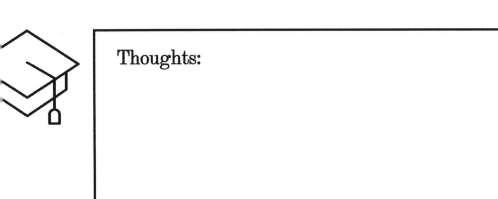

Thoughts:

Name:

Thoughts:

Name:

Thoughts:

Name:

Thoughts:

Name:

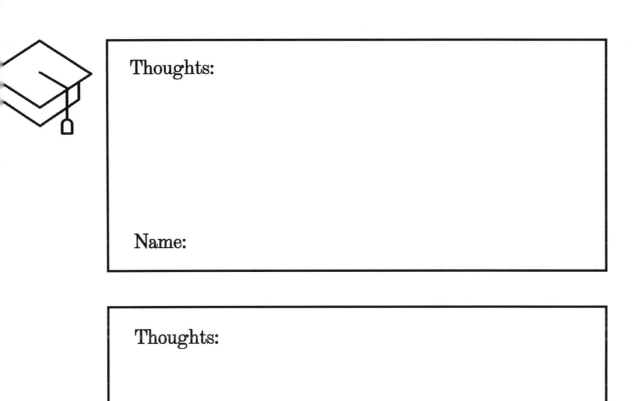

Thoughts:

Name:

Thoughts:

Name:

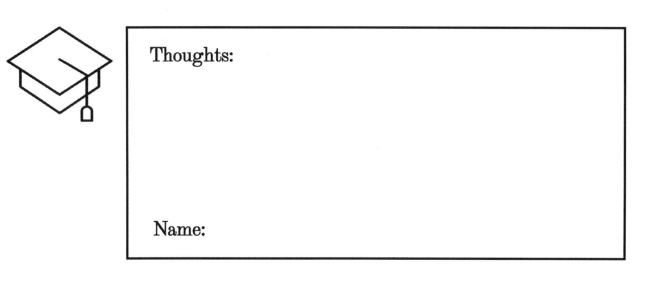

Thoughts:

Name:

Thoughts:

Name:

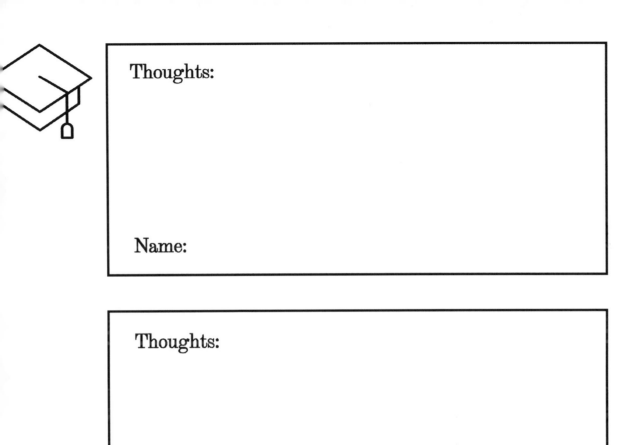

Thoughts:

Name:

Thoughts:

Name:

Thoughts:

Name:

Thoughts:

Name:

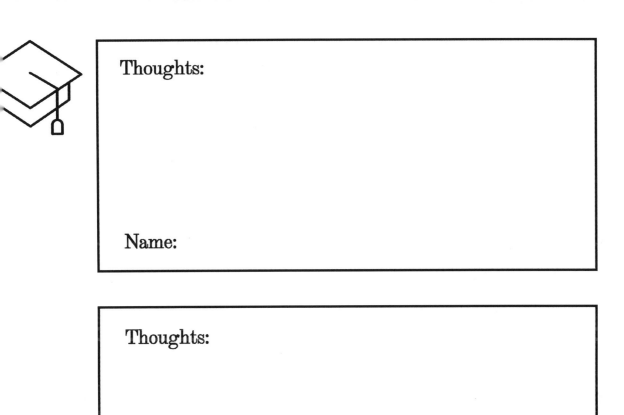

Thoughts:

Name:

Thoughts:

Name:

Thoughts:

Name:

Thoughts:

Name:

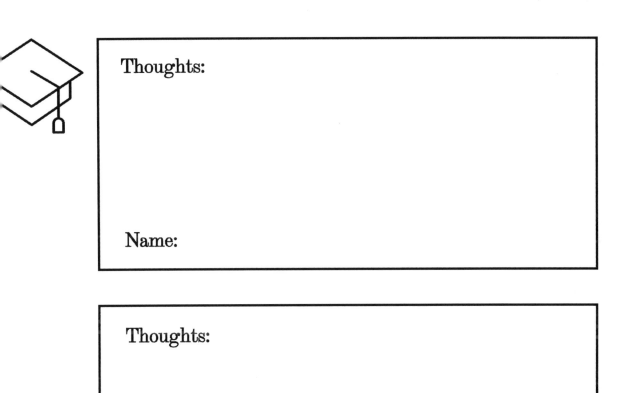

Thoughts:

Name:

Thoughts:

Name:

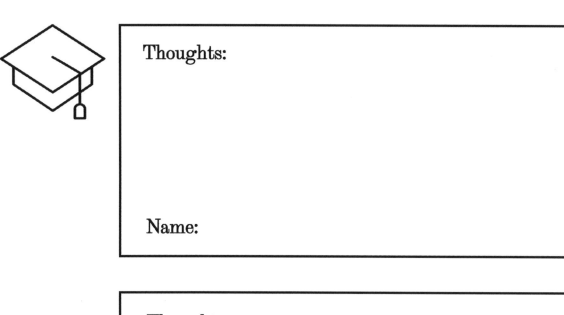

Thoughts:

Name:

Thoughts:

Name:

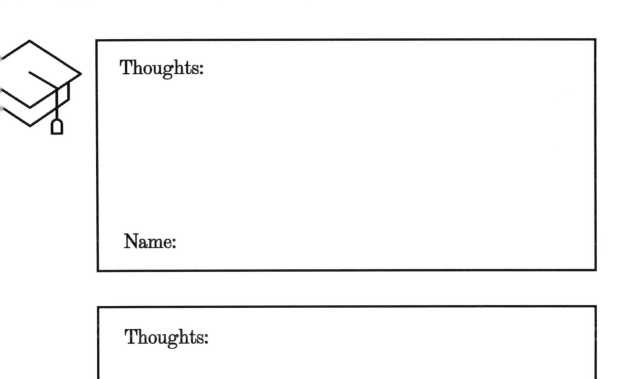

Thoughts:

Name:

Thoughts:

Name:

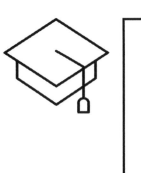

Thoughts:

Name:

Thoughts:

Name:

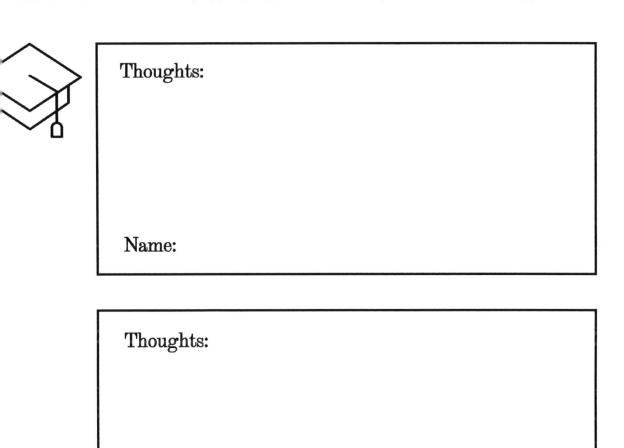

Thoughts:

Name:

Thoughts:

Name:

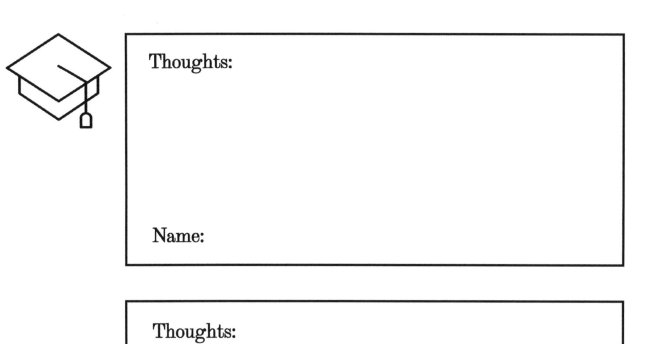

Thoughts:

Name:

Thoughts:

Name:

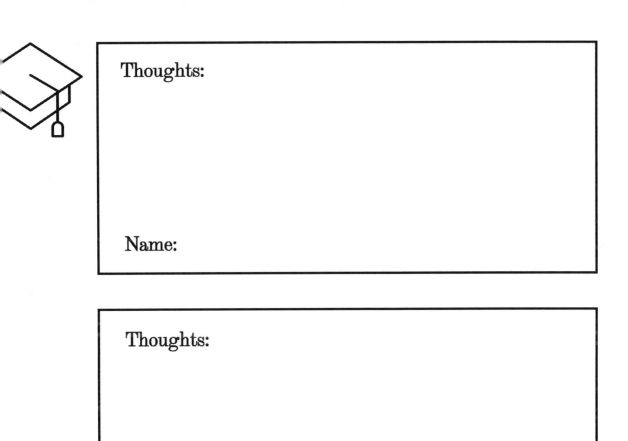

Thoughts:

Name:

Thoughts:

Name:

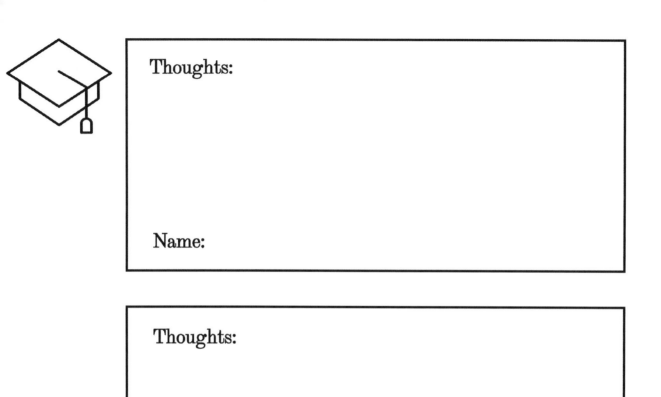

Thoughts:

Name:

Thoughts:

Name:

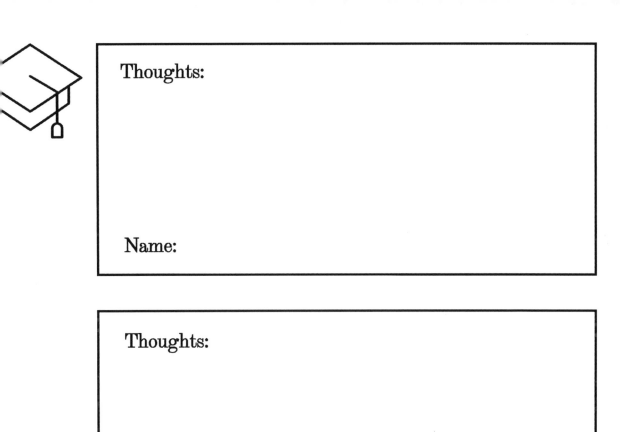

Thoughts:

Name:

Thoughts:

Name:

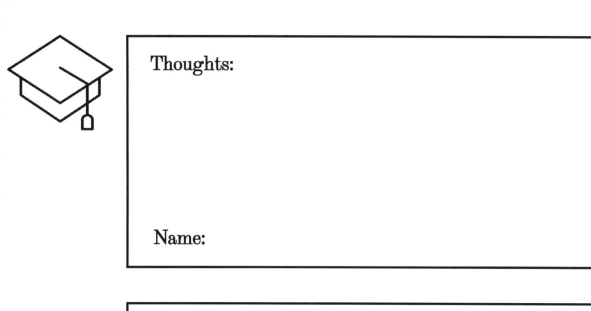

Thoughts:

Name:

Thoughts:

Name:

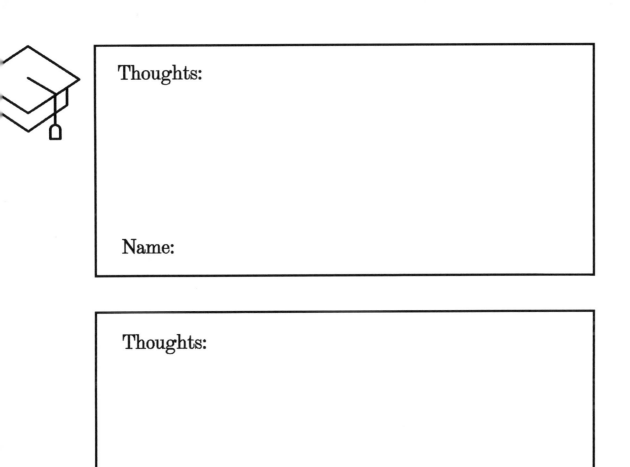

Thoughts:

Name:

Thoughts:

Name:

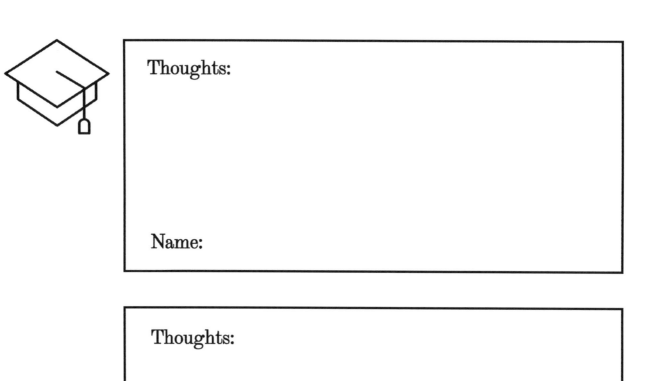

Thoughts:

Name:

Thoughts:

Name:

Made in United States
Orlando, FL
19 July 2022

19942952R10057